The International Work Experience

A Step-by-Step Guide to Working & Living Overseas

Glaisha A. Macarius, M.A.

Copyright © 2023 Glaisha Macarius

All rights reserved.

ISBN: **9798833663387**

Acknowledgments

Ithamar Macarius
For his continuous motivation, inspiration, and support of this book

Patricia Williams
For supporting my decisions to run around the globe

Richard Williams
For continuous support on every overseas contract

Glaister Atkinstall
For believing in me

Dedicated To

Dylan

Disclaimer

The information in this book is based on personal experience and opinion and does not guarantee that others will have the same experiences or similar outcomes.

The International Work Experience

The International Work Experience

Introduction

Post-secondary education is essential in our ever-changing and demanding society. Investing in a post-secondary or tertiary education creates more career options, and having more options is always a plus. Specifically, a 4-year or bachelor's degree will allow you to extend and build your professional experience overseas. It opens the doors to the possibility of being recruited to live and work in another country (maybe one you've always been fascinated with) and earning a good salary while doing so. This decision doesn't have to be long-term by any means, however, if you explore this option, even for a year, you will have the opportunity to experience things you never thought you would, and as oddly as it may sound, to experience what could feel like "The American Dream".

When exploring international career options, you must consider means to support yourself while overseas. Most overseas career opportunities that pay well enough where you can both save hefty and support yourself comfortably, will require a 4-year college degree with popular positions available in areas such as marketing, advertising, architecture, and education to name a few. The field of education, however, is a field

… that has one of the greatest demands on the international job recruiting front. While there are many available options within the field of Education to explore internationally (for example from positions such as Education Business Manager, Education Program Manager, Education Coordinator, Campus Director, and Human Resource Professional, to the positions of Teacher and Professor), most of the listing will be for teaching in some capacity. For most of the teaching positions posted, you likely will not need a degree in Education to be considered, but rather a bachelor's degree in any field. I will show you how to acquire these opportunities, even if your background, long-term career goals, and long-term interests fall within a different professional sector.

If your career goal is not to be a teacher or professor, but you are in a career transition, you want to take on a gap year, you're trying to figure out your next career move, or just simply trying to build your career, I would still recommend applying for a teaching position or any position in the Education field overseas.
It is also worth noting, that overseas employers who are recruiting in this field, are more prone to hire individuals from English-speaking countries and they typically focus on potential employees who are passport holders from the U.S., Canada, South Africa, England, Australia, and New Zealand. Now, this does not mean that if you hold a

passport from another English-speaking country, you are out of the running… not at all. But there is a strong focus on citizens from the above countries. So, suppose you are a passport holder from any of the above countries, or any other English-speaking country for that matter, and have a bachelor's degree in any field. In that case, you are pretty much a golden ticket for recruitment, especially for opportunities in Asia.

As I mentioned earlier, there are career opportunities across the board overseas, however, those in Education have some of the highest demand and therefore the most popular to acquire. Many of these opportunities are contracted by year, so you have the option of returning home or transitioning into another career field while overseas after a year, without feeling like you have abandoned the initial overseas employer too quickly. Further, accepting a teaching position or contract does have its rewards. I will discuss some of these advantages a little later, but I first want to highlight the prestige that Asian countries place on the teaching profession, on education in general, and on foreign teachers.

Being a Tutor, Teacher, Instructor or Professor is a highly valued and respected profession in Asia. Once a native person realizes your profession, their reaction typically reflects very high admiration—a slight contrast to how teachers are viewed in the U.S. for example,

The International Work Experience

though highly valued here. But imagine living in a society where, as a teacher, the reaction you receive is next to glorious. You may even get this reaction upon landing at the airport from the Customs and Immigration Officers themselves. This was my experience a few times, and I also recall several moments while teaching in Taiwan for example, when someone would ask me what I did for a living and when I told them I was a teacher, their reaction left me feeling a bit like Royalty. Even if you do not choose to take a teaching contract but something else in another field, there is a certain level of admiration that you will still experience as a Westerner living in Asia. That is, in and of itself, a very unique experience.

So, hold on to your hats, your curiosity is about to be fulfilled as I take you through a journey of information to help make your curiosity, dreams, interest, and your transition to living and working overseas, a true reality, and bring to light why this is one of the most memorable and most impressive career builders you could ever give yourself.

The International Work Experience

TABLE OF CONTENTS

Chapter 1	Why Go	3
Chapter 2	Finding Your Job	9
Chapter 3	Know Before You Go	25
Chapter 4	Arrival & Business	41
Chapter 5	Surviving Culture Shock	51
Chapter 6	Minding Your Manners	65

Conclusion

The International Work Experience

Chapter One

Why Go

One of the first reasons you should explore living and working overseas is simply because you owe it to yourself. Yes, you owe it to yourself to truly see and experience more of the world. To experience other people and a different culture is an invaluable experience and an amazing gift you could give yourself. It is also quite possible to experience how another culture accepts you, your background, and your credentials, is different from that which you may have experienced in your home country. That is, in a more extraordinary way. I recall while living in Taiwan, there were moments when I felt like a celebrity while out in the city because people wanted to take pictures with me and of me all the time. Being in different environments and cultures also broadens our view of the world and various issues, whether social, economic, religious, or political, and contributes highly to us being more open and accepting. I could go on and on in this respect, but in general, the opportunity to deeply experience another culture will contribute positively to being a well-rounded individual.

Now let me emphasize that there is a stark difference between visiting versus living. To be able to fully appreciate another culture and have a gainful experience, I suggest living there, whether it is short-term for 4 months or on a longer term for a year or more.

To be honest, it is easier to make the transition to live overseas when you are not moving with a large family nor have huge responsibilities like a mortgage or car note back in your home country. However, it is possible to do so under such circumstances, and there are many overseas teaching contracts out there that pay a huge salary and will accommodate families very well. However, it is an easier transition if you are an individual traveler with fewer responsibilities. Taking a contract, especially in Asia where salary offers are highest for overseas educators and other related roles, is a definite plus for those wanting to satisfy financial obligations. One financial obligation that some people who decide to live and work overseas face is that of their student loans. I have friends who decided to live overseas for four or five years in places like South Korea and Abu Dhabi for example and were able to pay off their student loans with salaries from those contracts; something they would not have accomplished in that same amount of time back in their home country. Low cost of living (in most cases), reduced responsibilities, living a cheaper lifestyle, and a good salary, are all factors that make this and other dreams possible while living overseas.

Another major advantage in deciding whether to live and work overseas is the opportunity to travel. Most people can fulfill their desire to travel to other countries while on an overseas contract. It is just easier. Here is the deal. As I mentioned, you will be able to save more based on the cost of living, salary, and adjusted lifestyle. As a result, most Expats teaching overseas are better able to arrange a trip to a place they have always dreamed of. I have spoken to many friends who have said, **"Had I not taken this job, I probably would have never gotten to see all these places."** I concur. While on my first contract in Taiwan, I was able to save and travel to Hong Kong, to Mainland China and see the Great Wall, to The Philippines, and Japan. Even if you do not travel to another country while on an overseas contract, just being in that country in and of itself and being able to visit that country's historical sites and attractions, is attainable and memorable. In addition to Taiwan, I have accepted contracts in other countries like France, Italy, and China. While on those contracts, I was able to visit and see the Eiffel Tower, the beautiful hills of Tuscany, medieval villages in Italy, the Roman Coliseum, and the Great Wall of China. It is a very cool experience to be able to earn a living and explore another culture all at the same time and in the same place. Think about it this way, when you accept an overseas contract, you are in a sense getting paid to travel. Truth check: Being able to make travel dreams to far places possible from living and working at home in the U.S. for example, may take a few years of savings just to visit one place; and that is likely if you're making a substantial and mature salary and have limited financial responsibilities.

    Now I've referenced a few Asian and European countries above, but I want to be perfectly honest and clear when I say if you are hoping to visit different countries while on your overseas contract, there is a greater possibility to do so with a contract in Asia versus that of Europe or Central and South America. The reason is that contracts offered in Asia typically have a higher salary. If you are making more money, you will be able to do more things. European contracts may not pay as much, though you will be able to save a bit and enjoy the beauty of the country in which you reside. Contracts in South America are merely sustainable; that is, you will be offered enough money just to sustain your way of life there. Most expats on South American contracts are primarily focused on a mission or cultural experience.

They are usually not looking to do much more financially. But if your dream is to travel and experience more places while on a single contract, I would recommend a contract in Asia.

Occasionally in life, we may find ourselves in a career transitional phase in one way or another. This applies to different people who are in distinct stages of their careers. Whether you are a university graduate trying to find a job, trying to decide whether to go to grad school, or trying to figure out how to transition into your career, or a career professional between employment, taking **an overseas contract can certainly help your career transition to be less difficult** and less stressful without the worries of having money. Not only can you utilize this overseas contract while thinking of the direction of your career or your next career move, but you can use this invaluable and impressive experience as a resume/career builder as well. Employers are typically impressed with professional experiences (whether seasonal, contract, or stop-gap) that show courage, the ability to adapt and fit in, the ability to perform job functions despite any obstacle (like language), and the ability to work in diverse environments or with diverse groups of people or simply shows that you kept on working. Overseas job experience will show the employer all the above and more about you as a professional. Additionally, you will have the chance to learn at least the basics of a foreign language while living in the culture and can add that language skill to your resume.

Here is an interesting fact: It could sometimes be easier to acquire a job overseas in the education and training industry than it could be when job searching in your home country. If you were to run this test yourself, you would see how quickly the overseas employers respond, and how soon an offer is made. I have been in career transition before, where after sending out countless resumes to employers in the city, and not getting much response, I decided to look state-wide and send out more resumes, and as those responses were slow as well, I decided to send resumes to employers nationally. When that also became frustrating, I decided to look at opportunities overseas. Within days of posting my resume, I was contacted by employers in Korea, Japan, China, UAE, Taiwan, Chile, and Africa who showed interest. After a quick and careful revision of the different jobs and offers, I signed a contract and was on my way to my new job in a matter of weeks. By the way, do not worry about how you will get there. **Most employers will include an offer to pay for your flight at the beginning and end of your contract.** Also, do not worry about obtaining a work visa for that country as the employer will take care of all of that for you and do so quite expeditiously. In my last contract with an employer in China, I received my airline ticket and work visa within a week after all paperwork and pre-employment requirements were completed. On a past contract to Taiwan, I was on a plane within three weeks of the time I received the job offer. My point is, if you ever find yourself in a frustrating job-search position, consider going international as a viable option. You may be able to lower the possibility of sitting at home stressed out month after month wondering when you will find a job as funds continue to deplete, as is sometimes the case with job search efforts at home.

    You will also gain strong friendships along the way. One of the most rewarding things that comes out of living overseas is the friendships formed with so many people from so many unique backgrounds. With social media, it is also much easier to stay connected and in touch after you have returned home. I am personally still connected to most people I have worked with overseas and have had quite a few of them serve as professional references for me throughout the years. Further, you will build business connections with people internationally. Having a global network connection can go a long way, especially if you are also thinking of doing any kind of business internationally at any point in your career. While I was working in Italy, I met someone who has a fashion agency and is interested in doing business together. We have also become particularly good friends. At the end of the day, you will form life-long friendships with people all over the world and will find the entire experience to be invaluable.

Write down three things you want to accomplish by taking on an overseas contract.

_____

_____

_____

Chapter Two

Finding Your Job

As mentioned previously, acquiring a job opportunity overseas can be a bit easier than most people think. There are hundreds of jobs posted online for overseas opportunities. It starts by simply browsing the internet. Remember though, that the dominant field will be in Education and Training and as you search you will see a lot of opportunities in that field. There are a lot of websites that will give you information on various job positions and where to find more of those positions. Just start browsing. Begin your search by typing in various key and search words such as jobs overseas, international job positions, education jobs abroad, international teaching positions, contract jobs overseas, etc. Any possible search will give you a list of results for you to further research. Some of the most popular sites or job boards for overseas opportunities in education are ESL Worldwide, The International Educator (TIE), Dave's ESL Café, Go-Abroad, Teach Away, Travel Abroad, and Teach Overseas.org. You may even find overseas opportunities on the Indeed and Career Builder job boards in any field as well. Because there are so many opportunities, the amount of recruiting and job posting sites is endless. So whichever one you choose for your research (even if it's not listed here), you will be sure to find an opportunity that meets your needs. Whenever I share with people that I'm going to work in a particular country they always ask with astonishment, "How did you get that opportunity?" They are always surprised when I say, "Oh I found it online and just sent them my resume." People are always asking how I got connected to the company, did I know someone, or was it through a school or work program? Not at all, I simply saw the job posting online and applied. That's all there is to it.

The question on your mind though is, "How will I know that these opportunities are legitimate?" Well, if it's any comfort, I am here to tell you from personal experience that they are. These companies, schools, and colleges are serious about recruiting professionals from the United States and other English-speaking countries. So, take a deep breath and let that sigh out. However, always do your research and be mindful. Here are some things to keep in mind after seeing a posting online:

(1) Do they have a website? It's a good idea to go to the company's website and read all about who they are. A website is a very credible place to start. (2) What

information are they seeking? Companies recruiting overseas will eventually need a copy of your passport page and a photo at some point in the contract signing. That is very normal and very necessary. However, they typically do not need information like your social security or bank account number. They will set up a bank account for you in that country once you've arrived so that your monthly salary gets deposited without any issues. If someone or any company is trying to solicit your social security or bank account number, <u>do not correspond with them</u>. Also, be sure to pay close attention to the person's name and professional title with whom you are doing most of your communication. (3) Review the contract documents carefully and pay attention to things like their use of company letterheads and copyright logos or lack thereof. If it looks like a random document a person quickly typed up in Word without any credible professionalism, then it probably is not credible, and they are therefore not as professional or authentic as they portray themselves to be. (4) Consider also, how big, or popular the company or school is, how professional they are in scheduling your first phone interview, and when you do the interview how they come across. How did they answer your questions in the interview? (Be sure to have questions as you would with any interview for a job position in your home country). The bottom line is to trust your instinct and research and investigate the company in the same manner you would normally when seeking a job opportunity. **One plus about working through popular recruiting sites is that they have already researched schools and colleges for you.** They have a reputation to uphold and so they are as careful who they represent to job seekers as they are who they recruit for placement with schools and companies. So, utilize a recruiting site like some of those mentioned previously, if that makes you more comfortable. But rest assured, most companies are very authentic in their recruitment.

To get the kind of position that you truly want, think about what you would like the most and be true to yourself in that process. If you think you will be better off working with adults or in a college setting, then narrow your search around that and focus first on those positions. Remember, *you* will be the person doing this job in a foreign country for a year or more, and while you can't truly tell the nature of the job until you are in the position, you want to make the best effort to ensure you won't be miserable doing something you don't like. Adjusting to another culture in and of itself can be challenging, you don't want to be in a miserable job position while going through a cultural adjustment. So, the approach I recommend in this process is to write down the top three settings or age groups you prefer to work with. If your number one choice is a college or university, start there for your country of choice. Then look to language or corporate companies with adult students, and then look to teenagers in an international school or language company. Typically, if you haven't worked abroad before in education, you won't know exactly how to filter what you want, so the best you can do is to thoroughly review the company or school and the job description and be honest with yourself about what you think you will be comfortable with.

Consider what you want from this experience. If you are more about the experience of another culture and less concerned about making and saving money, it is perfectly fine to include countries from Central and South America and Africa in your search. On the other hand, if your goal is to experience another culture and make and save money, then you may not want to include the above locations in your job search because the opportunities from these countries are less likely to meet those financial goals. What you can expect with those countries instead is to receive a salary offer that would be sufficient to sustain you while you are there and that's about it. If you are looking for a cultural experience and at the same time to save some money, then you may include European countries in your search. For contracts in Europe, you will enjoy the beauty of the culture and be able to put away a few coins; nothing significant to pay on a mortgage or student loans back home, but enough to allow you to travel to different sites and neighboring countries and be able to afford a return plane ticket home. If you choose to live in this region long term, you will have enough to sustain your way of life. Be aware though, that acquiring a long-term contract in Europe can be very tricky because of the hassle involved in work visa sponsorship in the European Union. If on the other hand, you are looking to make and save a lot of money while experiencing another culture, you want to look for opportunities primarily in Asia. That is the entire continent of Asia, from the Middle Eastern area up to Russia, over to Japan, and down to Singapore.

    Asia offers the highest salaries for these kinds of opportunities abroad. Additionally, most contracts to Asia include paid airfare and paid or stipend housing. You will hardly ever find a contract from South America or Europe that offers paid airfare and housing. Most of the opportunities from Asia offering paid airfare will offer roundtrip paid to the country and back home at the end of your contract. Sometimes you will see jobs that only offer the one-way paid airfare to the country, and that in and of itself isn't a bad deal either. But there are far more that offer round-trip paid airfare. Now the paid airfare back home is typically conditional on the fact that you complete your contract. If you break your contract, they will not pay for your return flight home. However, you most likely would have saved enough to where if you must break a contract (though not recommended) you will have money to buy your own ticket home. There may be some contracts out there in Asia that request that you buy the departure ticket from your home country and upon arrival in the contract country, you will be reimbursed. They do this as a security measure to ensure that if you accept the position, you will show up. I've experienced all the above types of offers with my work contracts overseas. I've been reimbursed for my travel, I've had my housing paid for, I've had a housing stipend offered, I've had round trip airfare paid, and I've even been on short-term contracts where both my housing and food were taken care of the entire time. Occasionally, you will see contracts where a car is thrown into the offer to aid in transportation. This is especially common in areas of Japan and the Middle East if your place of work is outside of their main metropolitan areas.

    Most contracts in Asia also offer an end-of-contract

bonus. So, if you sign a contract for a year, at the end of the year, you get a hefty bonus in addition to a paid departure flight. If you renew your contract for another year, you will also get another end-of-year bonus because each contract is treated separately. This end-of-year bonus is a wonderful thing and most expats overseas working on contracts with bonus offers typically look forward to it a lot as they approach each contract ending. Many people may even use their bonus as their airfare back home if they decide not to renew their contract or if that company doesn't offer paid return flights. Whichever way you choose to utilize your bonus, it is a nice benefit with these contracts in Asia.

Asia is also where you are likely to save the most money for travel. You will be able to save very quickly to book a flight to a neighboring country or a country you've always dreamed of visiting. I remember while I was working in Taiwan, I told myself I would not leave Asia without seeing the Great Wall of China, a site I've always wanted to see, and the funds to make that possible came very easily under my contract. I also was intrigued with Hong Kong and definitely wanted to visit. That dream also came true based on what I was able to save during my contract in Taiwan. I was able to visit the Philippines and Japan as well. All trips that would have been difficult for me to attain had I been back home in the United States trying to save up a dollar to make it happen. I also have many friends who have been able to make their travel dreams come true by working abroad. I have friends who have been able to visit places such as Egypt, Malaysia, Singapore, Jerusalem, Australia, and a whole list of other countries on these overseas contracts. They all say the same thing, "I would not have been able to see these places had I not taken a contract abroad." If, however, you are less interested in traveling on your contract and are more focused on saving or paying off financial obligations, as I mentioned earlier, contract offers in Asia could also make this possible.

It is good to know that International Schools in Asia are known to offer the highest salaries over colleges, universities, language schools, and corporate companies. With that being said, it is best to reflect on the teaching environment and contract you prefer ahead of accepting a contract and be willing to accept and stick with that company or school at least until that contract ends, no matter how enticing another offer may seem. It is never a good idea to accept one contract and switch contracts to another establishment after a couple of months. After all, the company did go through a lot of preparation to get you there; from arranging and paying for your travels, arranging your visa, getting you through training and onboarding, to helping you get set up with housing. Remember, you signed a year (or so) contract. Therefore, unless in extreme circumstances, you are expected to fulfill it.

It is also especially important to keep in mind the conversion rate and cost of living of the country of hire. Both factors work together and are important if you are aiming to save money. Japan for example is very expensive in terms of cost of living. So, you may need an offer close to what the industry offers in your home country or close to what you would have accepted in your home country to sustain a comfortable life there. When offered a salary for an overseas position, use an online currency conversion tool to let you know exactly what it is in U.S. dollars. For example, 298,802 Japanese Yen per month, may look like a lot of money, but by conversion, it's about USD 2,000/month. You will find that most, if not all contracts, will post what the position pays in monthly salary rather than yearly salary. Now if you receive a contract from a country that will pay for your flight (round-trip), pay for your housing, your utilities, give you an end-of-year bonus, and the cost of living for that country is low, a USD$2,000-3,000/month offer could seemingly be good. Due to adjustments in your lifestyle living abroad, coupled with the above benefits, you'd be surprised as to what you may be able to save from that amount of money. If you want to seek a contract that closely mirrors what you make in the U.S. as a teacher for example, a contract in the Middle East is your best bet, especially if you are a certified teacher with a master's degree. You will see a lot of postings for school-aged children in Middle Eastern areas like Qatar, Abu Dhabi, and Dubai that require teaching certification and a preferred master's degree. They do, however, compensate well to match their strict requirements.

Speaking of requirements, let's revisit what you can expect employers to want. So first and foremost, and as previously mentioned, **they will require at least a bachelor's degree**, most often in any field if you are looking into traditional schools, international schools, language companies, or private companies. At the college level, they will require a master's degree for a variety of positions and a Ph.D. for most university-level courses. In addition to the above requirements, you will often see "TEFL/TOEFL/CELTA certification preferred." These are certifications for teaching in English. Occasionally, you will see a position requiring one of these, however most often, if even listed in the job description at all, it will be as a "nice to have" but not a "must have." Do not be surprised if you see a position that only requires a bachelor's degree at contract signing but once on-boarded into the position requires that you complete one of those certifications above. In this case, the companies will most likely pay for the certification, but they will require you to attain it to continue employment with them. I have experienced this kind of "conditional" requirement with a contract I've accepted, and so I'm here to vouch that most companies will provide adequate time and support for you to achieve this required certification if necessary. Because I am an educator at heart, I thoroughly enjoy any course that will enhance my ability to be better at home or abroad. My suggestion is to embrace this kind of requirement and appreciate it as advanced education and professional development for your career.

You could from time to time see job descriptions that include age requirements. This is highly contrary to what we're used to in the U.S. and the rest of the Western world. However, these are different countries, and they have different rules. Sometimes you will see job descriptions that the applicant must be over 24 years of age; sometimes you will see job descriptions stating the applicant can't be over 55 years old. It all depends on the nature of the assignment and how *they* feel the applicant will or won't be able to carry out the job functions. Don't make a big deal out of it or be discouraged should you come across this kind of posting. If it doesn't relate to you go on to the next job. There are plenty.

As stated previously, the primary requirement and demand you will encounter is that you must be from an English-speaking country. While there are many English-speaking countries on the globe, regions like Asia tend to focus on applicants from New Zealand, Australia, England, The United States, Canada, and South Africa. You will see job postings requiring that you have a passport from one of the above. However, there are many contracts out there that look at the fact that someone may have grown up in and attained their college degree from one of these countries as a resident of the country but not a citizen, and they will often give these individuals the same consideration for employment. For some companies, being a "passport holder" or resident of an English-speaking country is not enough. They want to know that you are a "native" English speaker or that English is your first language. So, if you were born in Brazil for example, and migrated to the United States, became a citizen, and therefore have a U.S. passport, and you have a great command of the English language, but it isn't your "mother tongue", you may have to be convincing to get one of these contracts. If you believe your background may be misunderstood or unfairly evaluated, my suggestion is to make sure your resume is powerful and convincing to win you a phone or Zoom interview with an overseas school or company. If you get them to that point and can debunk any misconceptions, you have a pretty good chance of being on your way to a new adventure and cultural experience.

    Let's talk for a minute about visa sponsorship. If you are planning to work overseas for a length of time longer than three months, **you are likely to get a sponsored work visa**, regardless of the country you plan to work in and regardless of your citizenship status. The good news is there are lots of countries that make this process easy. The not-so-good news is that some make it a little more difficult. Let me begin by discussing a specific region that will make it a bit difficult to obtain a long-term work visa. While there are lots of opportunities in Europe, visa sponsorship for long-term and renewable contracts can be a bit of a hassle. This is because the governments of countries in the European Union have stricter policies, some of which are put into place to control immigration and refugee problems. This does not mean you should cross Europe off your list if your dream is to live and work there. What this means is that you really must research long-term opportunities and be prepared to submit a lot of paperwork for the company willing to do the sponsorship and be patient. You may face a longer preparation time to depart as they work a lot slower than the Asia region for example.

Asia on the other hand, will readily hand out work visa sponsorship to qualified candidates. This is because governments in this region (regardless of specific country) have made an intentional approach to diversify their education system. As a result, there are already certain factors in place by which companies, schools, and their government work together cohesively to bring talent into the country as quickly as possible. Their process is meticulous, careful, thorough, uniform, and "by the book." Make no mistakes about it. But they are also very swift with processing. I remember when I took my first contract job in Taiwan, I was on a plane within three weeks of signing the contract and had full permanent working residency within a month of arrival. When I signed a contract for an assignment in China, they processed everything on their end within two weeks and sent me the necessary paperwork to obtain the work visa from the consulate in the United States. I was granted a work visa within a week of sending that paperwork off and was sent my electronic plane ticket immediately once the company knew I had the visa. I was then on a plane within five days. Yes, that's how quickly they work. So, as you decide to embark on a career overseas, consider where you want to go, how quickly you would like to leave, and the likelihood of it happening in your desired time based on your country of choice. Sometimes some countries will do the bulk of the remaining paperwork processing after you have arrived in the country. If this is the case, do not worry, they have a certain system in place that allows the whole process to move very quickly upon arrival, and even more important to note, you won't have to deal with the stress of doing any of the paperwork because they do it all for you. Occasionally, you may have to travel to an office to sign paperwork already prepared for you but that's about it. You will observe that one day your manager or supervisor will hand over your passport with all the residency work stamps and permits without you knowing exactly when and how they completed it, and that's quite okay. Your job is to enjoy your experience.

FYI: Some overseas opportunities are short-term in nature (anywhere from 3-6 months) and therefore do not require visa sponsorship. These short-term contracts are prevalent in Europe and South America (though you will see a few in Asia), and I have also had the privilege of embarking on a couple of these assignments, where I spent a few months in France and Italy and got to grow my career through these unique opportunities. One of the good things about short-term assignments is that the company will cover your housing and, in some cases, meals and travel while on assignment. Sometimes, there is even the possibility to convert your short-term status into a long-term assignment if such a situation becomes available. If so, the company will do the necessary paperwork to make sure your status is updated. Normally though, once your short-term assignment ends, you will be expected to exit the country within the period granted in your passport on arrival.

Here's what to do and expect after you have reviewed a job in which you are interested. Send them all the materials they asked for in the job posting. Most often this includes your resume, a copy of your university diploma, a copy of your passport page showing the expiration date, and a photo. Again, as mentioned earlier, any company or person initially soliciting any information relating to a bank account number or social security number is not legit. Do not begin any process to work with them. Overseas companies will set up an account in their country on arrival for your salary to be deposited. Once they review your application materials, and they feel you are a good candidate, they will set up a phone or Skype interview with you very quickly. Pay close attention to the time they set for the interview and do not confuse their time and your time. For example, a recruiter or manager may say "We will call you at 8:00 am China time which will be 8:00 pm your time." They will most likely call you right on time, and just like a phone screening interview in your home country, you can expect this phone/zoom interview to last 30 – 60 minutes. Sometimes, there will be a second phone/zoom interview for a second round of screening. There is nothing much to suggest as far as doing the interview itself. The only general advice I would give is to remain as professional as you would, had it been a local employer conducting the interview. The same steps you would take in preparing for a normal job interview are the same steps you would take in preparing to speak with an overseas employer to get the job. Review and practice general and potential interview questions for the position. If it's a phone interview, make sure there isn't any noise disruption. If it's a Zoom interview, make sure your attire and background are appropriate. Don't worry about the language barrier too much at this point. Overseas companies will make sure the individual doing the interview speaks English proficiently. So, while this person may have a heavy accent, you will still be able to understand them very well and vice versa.

Once they decide to bring you on board and notify you of that, they will forward the employment contract to you. The contract will include the offers outlined in the job description as far as paid airfare, housing, monthly salary, whether utilities are paid, whether they are giving you a company car, end-of-year bonuses, the term of the contract, and your job title and functions of the job. It will also include additional information relating to your exact start date, benefits, paid holidays, vacation days, how you will be paid, medical insurance, what to expect if you renew your contract, as well as what to expect if the contract is broken. Read your contract carefully. Make sure that everything that attracted you to apply for the position is outlined in the contract and make sure that you are okay with any additional information stated. Overseas employers are incredibly open to answering any questions and meeting your needs before they put you on a plane to come to work in their country. So, ask as many questions as you need to after reviewing your contract so that you are truly clear about what to expect from the employer once you arrive in the country. You will likely sign your contract with an "electronic signature" at first and this is usually sufficient to bind the agreement between you and the employer and to move the hiring process along. Once you arrive in the country and have your first meeting (sometimes as quickly as the next day), you will re-sign those contracts with a hard signature, and both are kept on file. This was the case for all the work contracts I accepted overseas. For the companies I worked with, there was a next-day meeting for the contract signing, etc....., and I had a day or two after that to myself to settle in, get some rest, and begin to get over my jetlag before I began any workshops, onboarding, or training for the position. There is a possibility you will be given this time as well.

As mentioned above, after electronic contracts are signed, the school/company will then continue the hiring process in getting you to the country. They will go over information relating to a work visa, any prerequisite certification or training that needs to be completed before or after arrival, and when and how to expect your plane ticket (if offered in the contract). If there is a two or three-week gap in preparation from the time you sign the contract to the time you leave, rest assured that they will be in contact with you every step of the way to answer any questions and guide you along. **They are usually as excited about bringing another foreign talent on board as you are in exploring your talents overseas**, so they want to make sure that everything goes as smoothly as possible in getting you into the country.

Now that you have officially accepted an offer and have officially been given your start date, you will spend the next couple of weeks preparing for a change of life. Congratulations, you are officially on your way to the experience of a lifetime, stepping out of the box and broadening your horizon towards a greater dream.

Research and write down three recruiting sites you will use for your search:

1._____
2._____
3._____

Write down 2 preferred countries of choice:

_____

_____

Write down your foreseeable date of departure:

_____

Chapter Three

Know Before You Go

You have gotten your contract signed and sealed and are excited about embarking on this new career and cultural adventure. So now the preparation begins, and I hope to guide you through that process so that your transition can be as smooth and stress-free as possible. First thing, make sure to do additional research about the country, city, and company. You should have already done some research in these areas when conducting your job search and before signing your contract so that you have a good idea about who you will be working for and where you will live. By this point, you should have also already been at a particularly good comfort level based on the information you know so far. However, it's always best to get more detailed information to reduce any shock that may potentially come your way once you've landed in the country. So read as much as you can about the country and city to gain additional information about its history, its culture, people, population environment, climate, crime rate, economy, diversity, religious practices, etc. I usually print information from a few different websites and take that folder with me in my carry-on luggage when traveling. While in-flight, I like to re-read some of that information, and for me, it's like "comforted excitement." I also typically have my folder with my contract in my carry-on luggage as well and would read it over while in-flight.

It is a good idea to invest in a small pocketbook or its digital version, which details the country's cultural practices and norms, and that explains what is deemed acceptable and unacceptable in their culture. This is another item to add to your checklist that will help pass your time on what will likely be a very long flight. Being informed and having an open mind in adopting these cultural norms will likely reduce the potential of offending anyone, will help avoid a lot of misunderstandings, and will make your transition much more enjoyable. For example, while on my way to China during one contract, I learned it was considered disrespectful to hand over something with one hand and it was not in 'good taste' to point using one finger but instead to gesture to something with the entire hand. While reading up before going to Japan I learned it was offensive to offer tips. While many natives would realize that you are not from the country and may silently excuse an action that isn't culturally acceptable, many others would appreciate the fact that you try to blend into their culture by conforming to their norms and practices.

A grammar pocketbook would be equally useful at this point as well, especially if you are not proficient or fluent in the country's language. Of course, you shouldn't be concerned about memorizing everything in the book but review those useful phrases to help you get around. Some target situational phrases that I recommend starting with are: Can you help me, phrases on how to order the basics of your favorite foods, asking how to find a common facility (bank, grocery store, pharmacy, police station, train station), phrases on giving directions (useful for a cab driver), knowing how to count and say their currency. So, when you are about 7 hours in-flight and you've already read over contracts and information about the country and city, reach for that grammar/phrase book before you begin your in-flight sleep.

From the very moment your electronic plane ticket is sent to you, it makes everything real and solidifies the fact that you have accomplished something wonderful and will soon be on your way to a great experience. There is some key information to keep in mind as you get those suitcases together for your life-changing adventure. I will outline a few suggestions that will certainly help in your transition and reduce the chance of becoming stressed out upon arrival. First, **never assume that you will be able to buy whatever additional item you may need upon arrival, just for the sake of traveling light.** To make that assumption is to think that other countries may have the same set-up and flow as the United States or your home country when it comes to the availability of goods and services. This is usually not the case, and you may not be able to find the specific brand of something that you're used to so easily. My advice is to pack all the basics that will carry you over for at least three months. Start with a few pairs of work pants, shirts/blouses, a sweater, a jacket, a couple of pairs of shoes for work, and a work bag (or something additional to your pocketbook). Remember in the last chapter I mentioned that upon arrival most companies will have a meeting the next day and begin their training and on-boarding process almost immediately? This means you may not have a lot of time to browse around and go shopping for things within the first few days of arrival. Therefore, pack all the essentials, especially to be able to go to your meetings right away looking appropriate and feeling comfortable. Additionally, sometimes the training schedule and onboarding are so busy and rigorous that you may not even have time to go shopping for about another week. You will also be jet-lagged in the process and chances are you will want to sleep in on your first couple of days off. I will say this now and reiterate it as we move through the additional chapters, **the key is to pace yourself.** You could get overwhelmed very quickly in a new country, with a new job, and with the demands of the job and the way they do things on the job in that country. So, pace yourself from very early. One way to help achieve a good pace is by being prepared with essential items and clothing on arrival and not having to worry about trying to get something you need for basic functioning within the first week.

If you have accepted a contract in Asia, there is even more of a reason to pack your primary pieces of clothing for everyday functioning, including work. Why? Because it is extremely difficult to find clothing items in Asia that fit most Westerners unless you are a size 7 or under. If you figure to yourself that you will "only pack one pair of pants for work and just buy a couple more pairs after you get there," you will run the risk of possibly wearing that same pair of pants all week. The Asian population is naturally smaller in stature than Westerners, so shoes and clothing sold there naturally appeal more to local consumers. If you wear size 9 shoes in U.S. measurements and are larger than a size 8 in clothing, it will be more difficult for you when buying clothes and shoes. When I took contracts in Asia, this was something I was always mindful of and well prepared for. I experienced some frustration in buying clothes and shoes as I fell within those measurements above, so most of the shoes I tried on were just a bit too small and most pants and shirts were too snug. The funny thing is, while I may have been a bit frustrated and disappointed with the lack of proper fittings, the sales associates on the other hand did everything in their power to help me get fitted or somehow convinced me that the obviously below size garment fitted me well. This I found to be quite amusing. When I wanted to go shopping, I had to make sure I blocked out a few hours to have the time to go from place to place and try on multiple clothing. On a scheduled shopping day, I would also travel to a large shopping mall where I was more likely to find some Western sizes (and even then, there is a possibility you could run into the same difficulty). While these larger shopping malls in comparison to small neighborhood stores and shopping centers may have larger sizes, be aware that they will also be more expensive.

If you accept a contract in Europe, Africa, or Central & South America, finding sizes that fit won't be as difficult. But again, the time factor to go shopping within that first week or two will likely be an issue, so make sure you are as prepared as previously discussed. While it may be cheaper to buy clothing in parts of Asia, it could be more expensive to do so in parts of Europe. Therefore, unless you are arriving with a good handful of financial savings, pack wisely. While many expats making this transition may have a little bit of savings on arrival, most depend on their first salary deposit to aid them in their transition. With any of the regions discussed, be sure to also check out what the season and weather look like as you pack and how it will look over the next couple of months. You don't want to arrive in a city where it's cold for example and you don't immediately have a jacket handy. Take a few items of clothing for the change of season as well. You could arrive in the cold months and as it got warmer you may have a challenge finding T-shirts and sandals right away that fit, depending on your country of choice.

Packing all essentials of course also includes toiletries and personal grooming products. The same concept and suggestions also apply here as outlined above with clothing. That is, never assume that you will be able to find an item of choice right off the plane. Pack enough personal products to carry you over for at least two months. An additional reason to pack your suitcase with these items is the fact that you may not be able to read or decipher the information on the packaging for products in that country, at least for a while until you begin to figure things out. If you accept a job offer in a country that speaks a language other than English, you could very well run into this barrier. Sometimes in big and popular cities, you may find some English on products, but for the most part, Items will be packaged in the country's native language. Also, if you are not fluent in the language to explain certain details of the product to the sales associate, they may not be able to help you choose the right product. While you may be able to make an educated guess in countries that use the alphabet and sometimes have similar-sounding words in their language, like Spanish and French for example, you will have a much harder time figuring things out in countries that do not use the alphabet system but use completely different characters as in Arabic, Greek, and Chinese.

So, suppose you can't read, decipher, or explain the product information right away. In that case, I strongly recommend packing those basic and essential personal products until you can figure out where to find them in the city/neighborhood you will reside in or until you can figure out the correct product you desire. This has often been my experience while working overseas when I need to replace products I arrived with. It was also my experience when I needed other products that were too heavy to take in my suitcase. This part of my experience was always an adventure to remember. I can recall while living in Mainland China and Taiwan for example, I would go to the store to get detergent, softener, and bleach. I would be confused as to which was which because I could not read Chinese characters, and the packaging and shape of the container all looked the same. Now over time, I was able to differentiate the bleach from the detergent and softener, but being able to figure out the softener from the detergent was a whole different story. There are so many adventurous examples like these that I could give, but I'll allow you to experience it for yourself. The point is to be as prepared as possible with the grooming items you're used to (moisturizers, lotions, bath & hair products, toothpaste, etc....) to reduce stress as you begin your training and work. That way, when it comes to getting the heavier household items that you couldn't have packed, you'll be able to appreciate the adventurous and memorable moments of the experience rather than getting upset about it because you were already stressed from the day before when you couldn't find your preferred moisturizer.

Ladies, take my advice and pack feminine products that work best for *you;* enough to last you at least three months. Save yourself the headache of being uncomfortable. You are likely to run into the same issues as I outlined above, of not being able to find the brands that suit you quickly enough, or if you do, not being able to read and choose the specific product that works best for you. I also guarantee that you are unlikely to find your favorite brand as well. Take enough products with you to give yourself enough time to explore and research where to find similar items and which of that country's brands works best for you. Just for your information and speaking from my experiences, some Asian countries, specifically larger, more populated Asian cities, are less likely to actively market, sell, or have flushable absorbencies readily available to consumers. I was told one of the reasons for this may be to better protect their drains. So, take my advice and stock up so that you feel comfortable and secure to give your new overseas work adventure your absolute best!

Medicines are additional items I also recommend packing when going on your contract, and I would say pack enough of the medicine you think you may need to last you at least a couple of months. With medicines, you will face the same issues I talked about earlier and if your contract is in Asia, you most definitely want to travel with a bottle of your 'go-to' meds. This is because the medicines in Asia are quite different from the U.S. and the Western region. For one, many Asian countries use herbal medicines. As a result, the medicines available over the counter in their pharmacies are primarily herbal medicines. These medicines, while effective, are very slow in the healing process. You will also find some non-herbal medicines as well, but these will also be weaker in strength in comparison to Western medicines. In some pharmacies (very far and in-between in Asia) you may also see medicines with familiar Western brand names like Tylenol and Robitussin for example. But even these are manufactured in the country and will not be as strong as the ones you would normally consume at home. The Chinese people, for example, do not believe in a quick and sudden fix but a gradual progression to healing. So, you will find that all their medicines take on this progressive effect. If you are not used to going about it this way in the healing process, I would recommend bringing whatever will help your transition to be comfortable. If you know that there are certain medicines you usually have on hand if you suffer from migraines, bring your go-to meds to knock them out. If you know that there are certain meds you rely on every month, then throw a bottle in your suitcase. This is just until you get settled and figure some things out, such as the closest pharmacy, which pharmacy carries western-type meds, and which of their medicines works best for you and your situation. Trust me, you'll thank me for this advice later. I have quite a few personal experiences I could share as they relate to what I describe here. There was this one moment in particular when I had minor surgery in China, and after being out of surgery and in excruciating pain, they did not have, nor did they practice using the heavy dosage of post-surgical pain meds we have in the U.S. Thankfully, I had a bottle of ibuprofen in my handbag that I had packed when traveling over, and I was able to take doses (with their approval) over the next few hours to help ease the pain. Don't get me wrong, the doctors were great! They were specialists and were very attentive to my needs and wanted to do everything they could to get me through the post-surgery period. But the medicines they had just weren't doing it for me. So, the moral of the story is that when you decide to live abroad, pack those meds as you never know when they will come in handy.

It is probably a good idea to take what I would call "comfort items" with you as well. I am talking about anything that typically helps you to relax in your own space. I loved watching the comedy series Seinfeld, and in my daily routine at home in the U.S., I would get home from work and watch a couple of episodes as I unwind from my day. So, what did I do when I was preparing for my overseas job? Well in my earlier contracts, I packed a couple of Seinfeld DVDs in my suitcase and was incredibly happy that I did. Towards my later contracts, I would download episodes before arrival to ensure I had immediate access to Seinfeld episodes. While there is so much to experience and see, and so many new friends that you will make, you will have moments of feeling a little homesick, especially in the earlier months of arrival. If you have items that are a part of who you are and help you to feel better, it makes the transition that much easier. So, print a couple of pictures of friends and family, download your favorite TV show, and songs, and make sure to take a favorite book or two.

    Another reason to pack those comfort items is the fact that you may not have access to the internet immediately upon arrival. It may take you a while to get this set up. Not all countries and businesses in foreign countries operate within the fast-paced nature that countries like America do. Here in America for example, it is usually as simple as calling the phone and Internet company, they will quote packages available, you make your choice and set a date for installation and set-up, which is usually pretty quick. In another country, internet set-up can become a whole process that takes time. Even if you had someone who speaks the language to do the communication with the company for you, several issues could come up to delay your set-up. It must have taken me a month or so to get my internet set up in my apartment in China. I remember the process being complicated initially, and dates for which connection could be set up took weeks. During this time, I relied on the Internet at work. Additionally, in some Asian countries, you will be blocked from the Western internet. China is a good example of this kind of internet blocking. China's internet blocking is infamously known as "The Great Firewall of China" because you will not be able to access many Western social sites like Facebook, Twitter, Instagram, and YouTube from their internet. To gain access to the Western internet and subsequently these social sites, **you will likely have to purchase a VPN** or Virtual Pin Number. A VPN routes your computer as if you were using it in another country and city. That is, although you are using a computer in China, it could register as Houston, TX for example. This will allow you to utilize the internet as if you were back in your home country. When I finally got my internet connection in my apartment in China, my next step was to get a VPN, so I could be connected to the virtual world to the west. By talking to other friends and coworkers about a VPN, you will gather enough information to know the best ones to use and how to get it.

With all that being said, you will need those "comfort items" until you can get set up and completely settled, and until you can post that first picture to your social media showing everyone back home the amazing journey and opportunity you were offered and are experiencing. While I've made these suggestions to help in a comfortable transition, you also want to be mindful of how much you're packing. The last thing you want to do is have an overweight suitcase or an extra suitcase than is allowed for an international flight. Take heed, this will cost you an arm and a leg! Check with your airline early to get information on rules relating to international travel and their general baggage fees. While you want to pack wisely for a smooth transition, you don't want to pack foolishly and spend a lot of money out of your arrival budget because you have to pay extra baggage fees. This brings me to my next point……

Like Mama always says, "Never go anywhere without a little pocket change." While your first paycheck off the plane will be speedy (generally a standard week or so), you don't want to rely solely on that for initial set-up. While your arrival budget does not have to be a whole lot of money because the company will likely pay for your transportation from the airport, pay for your hotel or apartment on arrival, take care of your meals for the first few days, and depending on the contract may even have an apartment set-up for you and utilities connected, you still need to have a decent amount in "transition money". Just for security and to take care of a few things that might come up before your first paycheck from the company. I would recommend at least USD 300 or its equivalent if you are from another country. You will have the opportunity to do a currency exchange at the airport, but in the event, you don't get the opportunity to do so, your company Director will certainly help you with the currency exchange. Here are some little things to be mindful of in which having an arrival budget comes in handy. While most companies will pay for food on arrival, it most certainly will be three scheduled meals, so you want to be able to buy snacks throughout the day as well or have something for a night snack if necessary. You may also need to invest in an international phone card on arrival (which company representatives will help you get) if you are not able to use your home cell phone internationally, and until you get your local cell phone set up. Some companies will eventually provide you with a cell phone. Some may ask for a deposit to get your phone set up, and some may not. For those who do not provide a cell phone, they will help you get one set up and if you are trying to do so before the first paycheck it is good to already have a little cash on hand. Cell phone set-up is typically easy and cheap so do not worry.

If there is additional visa processing required upon arrival, you may be asked for a small fee here and there for final document processing which may be before your first paycheck. So, you want to have money available for that. Most companies are clear about outlining what you can anticipate in the first week and any money that may be associated with things that need to be done. So again, read everything in the contract and/or ask as many questions as you need to before arrival. Throughout my contracts, and depending on the country, I encountered paying for additional passport-size pictures, residency visa processing, snacks, dinners with new friends and colleagues, and a cell phone, all before that first paycheck arrived. So, to reiterate, about USD 300, or its equivalent in pocket money, should be sufficient to aid with any initial expense on arrival.

Finally, make sure you double-check to ensure you have all the necessary documents with you pertaining to your contract. You will of course have your

I.D., passport, and visa if applicable, but make sure you have the original copies of all documents requested by the company. If the company began the work visa processing before your arrival, then make sure you have all the documents they sent you which may include the official offer letter and a letter from the Department of Labor, Immigration, and/or Education. Of most importance, **make sure you have the contact information** (preferably the phone number) **of the person at the company you have been communicating with** and any other individual's number that was given to you as part of the arrival process. This is extremely important to have in your possession on arrival so that in the event there are any unlikely mishaps you will know exactly who to contact immediately. Speaking of mishaps, I encountered quite a little mishap on my first overseas work contract to Taiwan, but luckily, because I had these important contact numbers with me, I was able to resolve it without losing my mind. What happened was on arrival in Taiwan, I knew (per instructions in my contract) to look for a representative of the company holding my name on a card as soon as I cleared and exited baggage claim. Well, there I was, pushing my cart with two suitcases out of customs/baggage claim and walking by a long line of people waiting to greet arriving passengers. I was sure to pay close attention to each person holding a sign and as I cleared the exit area, I noticed I didn't see anyone holding my name. I decided to backtrack my steps and look again, but I still did not see my name. If I recall correctly, I must have walked back and forth through that area about four times. I immediately went into panic mode, as it dawned on me that I was in a foreign country, it was my first time in this country, I didn't know anyone, it was nighttime (my flight arrived somewhere around 8:00 pm), and I didn't speak the language, someone was supposed to pick me up and they were not there. Talk about Panic!

    Luckily, I had my contact person's number on hand, and I went over to the information desk and asked to make a call. Well, the story doesn't end there. While this company had late office hours and was able to get through to someone at the company, there was a bit of a language barrier, and they didn't quite understand what I was talking about. This sent me into double panic mode. Eventually, someone else came on the phone and was able to understand but told me that my primary contact had already left the office which immediately sent me into triple panic mode. The person on the phone did her absolute best to reassure me everything would be okay, and she went into problem-solving mode herself by attempting to contact the Director at home.

Eventually, they called back at the airport information desk and after speaking with the Director we realized there was a mix-up in the day and time communicated by the 3rd party recruiter. The Director immediately arranged for the airport shuttle to take me to the airport hotel, arranged and paid for my overnight stay at the hotel with meals, and immediately arranged for my pick-up in the morning. Now by this time, I was a bit more relaxed and the moment I got into my hotel room I was all good. The next morning, I was picked up in a nice executive car and went to meet the Director. Funny enough, we became good colleagues and to this day we are good friends, and we often reminisce and laugh over 'the airport incident.' While my experience here was unique and rare, I wanted to drive home the importance of having those contact numbers on hand upon arrival in the event something doesn't go as smoothly as expected.

    Now that you have all the "knows" and are packed and prepared, it is time to get those goodbyes in with friends and family as you embark on this exciting and unique opportunity.

Complete a checklist of important transitional items.

- Further research about the country, city, and company
- Pocketbook about culture
- Pocketbook basic phrases
- A few pieces of clothing for work
- Personal grooming products
- 'Go-to' meds (if applicable)
- Comfort items
- At least USD 300 or its equivalent
- Work contract and other work documents
- Contact person's name & phone number

The International Work Experience

Chapter Four

Arrival & Business

Thirteen hours, five movies, three meals, and two glasses of wine later (if that's your thing), you have landed in a country for a new adventure that you've been excited about, and it finally hits you that you are here! Take a minute, capture the moment, and take it all in. After regular business with immigration and customs, the only thing that will be on your mind is to exit the airport to finally see and explore this country and this new opportunity. As stated in your contract, a representative will likely be waiting to greet you with a name sign. This will be the first true moment of interacting with a company representative in person, so though you may have just gotten off a long flight, greet them with a friendly face as they will be delighted to meet you. You can expect this company representative to be proficient in English but in the event, they are a bit limited, do not be thrown by their silence, as it's not directed at you, but rather that they may not feel confident enough with their English to engage in a full conversation. They will be very friendly however and will likely offer to take your bags for you. They will insist on pushing your luggage cart out to the car, and the representative and the driver will load your luggage for you. **You are likely to be picked up in an executive car** and will be able to enjoy the lovely ride into the city in comfort. As a side note here, please also be aware that on some short-term European contracts, they may outline the train or airport shuttle bus to get on once you have arrived, and a representative will typically meet you at your destination stop. This is quite common with short-term European contracts.

Once your car has arrived at the destination, you will probably be escorted to your permanent apartment, transitional apartment, or hotel, depending on your contract. A different company representative typically meets you at that time to greet you, help you get settled in, and tell you what the plans are for the next day. This is most likely a director or manager that you will be working with either through the onboarding process or directly in your actual role at your company or school. Take your time and get some rest to begin getting over your jetlag, as you will probably be up the next day meeting more of the team and getting additional paperwork taken care of. You are unlikely to get an extra two or three days to 'settle in' and get over your jetlag.

These companies and these kinds of contracts typically move very quickly in getting you to work as soon as you get off the plane. So again, you want to be prepared with enough clothing and grooming items on arrival as there will be no time to shop. You may want to use this time to organize some clothing and grooming items in preparation for the next day, as well as any pertinent documents they are requesting for the meeting that day. You may also want to take this time to make the necessary phone calls to loved ones back home to let them know you have arrived safely, and all is well. If you do venture off the premises, make sure not to go too far so soon on arrival but to stay within the surrounding areas. The last thing you want to do is heighten your anxiety and stress yourself out the night before your first official meeting because you got lost.

Unlike the whole executive car ride and royalty treatment you would have enjoyed on arrival from the airport, on day two of arrival you will most likely have to find your way to the office to begin business. They are most sure to communicate with you exactly how to get there of course, but you will pretty much be on your own following those directions and instructions. This was the case with all my overseas contracts. When I arrived in Taipei, I remembered the Director giving me directions to the main office in the city center where I would complete additional paperwork on the third day. Similarly, after arrival in Paris on a contract to France, I along with a couple of other new teachers were greeted by one of the recruiting Directors and were given directions to take a train from Paris to the onboarding site in the south of France the following day. I also had to find my way from Rome to an onboarding site south of Naples for my contract in Italy and recalled myself and three other employees making our way through Shanghai a couple of days after arrival to begin formal orientation and onboarding for our contract in China. You get the idea. It is not unusual to be placed in a very independent position very quickly. While being in this position can sometimes be a little daunting as the fear of getting lost in a country where you may not be fluent in the language looms in your head, on the other hand, it's quite adventurous and after just the first travel in and around the city, you will begin feeling like a pro in navigating your way around.

    The paperwork process and training schedule are usually busy, but smooth. You will likely be re-signing contracts in hard copy and filling out additional documents that relate to work and work clearance. They usually make additional copies of your passport and diploma and usually have you open your bank account, get your cell phone, and take any additional passport photo for further work permit processing. Usually, the representative completing this orientation process with you will likely take you to lunch at a nice authentic cultural restaurant all on the company's tab. Use this time to further bond with them and if you have other employees starting in the same role at the same time as you, this is a good time to begin getting to know them as well. Remember, while you are getting ready to enjoy a cultural experience **your goal should also be to begin building an international network**. Talk to each other, exchange information, and once settled into your job, invite them out a couple of times, even if you all will be working at different locations/campuses.

    Just like any typical orientation process in your home country, you will be taken to your work location and introduced to the team. This may be on the same day that you complete the paperwork described above or could very well be the following day. The Director will show you exactly how to get to work from where your home is likely to be and usually takes the time not only to show you around the company but also around the neighborhood where you will be working so you may get familiarized with the area before your actual first day of work. It is also very typical of them to show you a few stores and markets close to where you live so that you can find certain things within reach as you settle in. As early as the first couple of days or first week, I would strongly recommend ensuring they have your emergency contact back home. I would also recommend you write down the employer's contact information for your contacts back home and have a translated copy in the country's language in your wallet or pocketbook. I also recommend getting to know what the emergency number is for that country within the first week. For example, In the U.S. the emergency dial is 911, while in Taiwan the emergency dial is 119. It's a good idea to have this kind of knowledge and awareness. Additional information that I believe is smart to have handy are the numbers for the local police and the number and location of the U.S. Consulate in your city. Keep these numbers handy in your wallet and on the wall or refrigerator in your home. These suggestions are not to bring fear to you or scare you in any way, nor to suggest anything negative about the country in which you will be residing. Rather, I include these suggestions to help you think of important information you should have when living abroad.

    In some cases, after meeting and touring with your director or orientation coordinator, you may have an extra day off. If you do, use it wisely to sleep and get over your jetlag as the formal onboarding process will likely begin the next day. I know that it is very easy to get caught up in the excitement of a new life and culture and therefore may want to party and have fun with the equally excited. But I caution you to pace yourself so soon on arrival. It will not be the best decision or in your best interest to be going non-stop so soon and wanting to follow your new colleagues everywhere they want to go at this point. As I reiterated a couple of times prior, **pace yourself for the training schedule to follow.** You signed a year's contract, so believe me, you will have plenty of time to go out, socialize, and see all the different places you want to. A quick stop at a pub once or twice on the onboarding schedule is okay, but beyond that, you may be doing too much too early, and could potentially burn out which will cause you to be stressed out. This could potentially cause you to get sick very early as well. Remember your body is adjusting to a new time zone and new kinds of foods so take it easy.

Formal onboarding usually will be busy and rigorous. It is not unusual for the school or company to try to pack everything they think you need to know and become proficient with, into one week. So, we are talking about something that looks like a 9 to 5 schedule and in some instances longer. They will predictively go over everything from cultural norms, and cultural taboos, to the technical stuff such as curriculum and lesson plans, as well as soft skills necessary for you to be successful in your role at their company or school, and their culture. After each training day, take the time to go over and process the training materials and handouts and prepare for the next day while making sure you're eating a good meal as well. **Eating well is extremely important in this type of transition.** Your body is adjusting not only to a new time zone but in some cases to a new climate, new kinds of foods, and new times to eat. It is not unusual for someone on a new contract going through these kinds of changes to get sick within the first three weeks of arrival, and it could very well happen to you. Although I was very mindful of my diet and very good at pacing myself and my schedule, within a month of arriving in Taiwan, I got a little sick because of the new adjustments and also had an allergic reaction to seafood (which I've never had before). Within a couple of weeks of being in Italy, believe it or not, I reacted to the heat which caused my foot and ankles to get swollen. Both instances gave me my first visit to the Doctor's/Pharmacist in the country. Certainly though, if you stay mindful of pacing yourself and eating well, it may decrease your chances of you getting sick during the early transitional weeks.

Your eating habits and diet will change as soon as you arrive. From my experience, because of these changes in diet, most individuals on a new overseas contract experience changes in their weight as soon as the first couple of months and during their contract term, most often on weight loss. This may or may not be an advantage to some, but such a change is likely imminent. For me personally, every time I took an overseas contract, I lost a few pounds and that isn't something I necessarily complained about. Also, as far as changes in diet, you will likely experience from your first few grocery shopping outings that you may not be able to find the exact kind of ingredients or seasonings that you have from back home in your home country. You will run into this a lot, especially in Asian countries. But if you keep an open mind and find similar substitutes, then you will still be able to cook and enjoy your favorite meals and may even develop an appreciation for a new taste. I encourage you to also have an open mind to the culture on arrival. If you arrive to live and work in a country, but then you are constantly comparing everything around you and every situation to 'home', then I am here to tell you that you will likely become very frustrated very quickly. It is important to remember that you are now in an entirely different country with different rules, laws, practices, behaviors, and foods.

It is also illogical to accept a contract to live in a country and expect them to follow *your* rules. Be respectful and open to the fact that you are now in their country, so you should follow their rules. I can't stress this enough. I've seen so many professionals who take a contract expecting things to be as they are used to in their home country, only to get frustrated and sometimes even become rude to local citizens and authorities when they must now abide by different rules and norms. It is not a good idea to arrive and settle in with this kind of tone, nor to continuously display this kind of behavior throughout your time living there. To be honest, this kind of behavior reflects negatively on the native people. I assure you that **most native citizens are excited about who you are and will go out of their way to help you with kindness.** They are usually very accommodating to the fact that you may not speak their language fluently to communicate with them well and they will often go out of their way to find someone who knows a bit of English so they may communicate with you. From my experiences, I'm often blown away by how many people get frustrated at natives for not understanding what they are saying in English and for not being able to speak English, when in fact as foreign residents in their country, we should be the one making an effort to learn to communicate in that country's language. My advice is to travel around with a phrase/vocabulary book if you must, try to be patient with yourself and local citizens, and show appreciation when they offer to help you, even if it takes them a few minutes to do so. This open mindset will most definitely work in your favor within the first couple weeks of arrival and long-term throughout your contract.

      As you begin to get settled, you will probably be finalizing your apartment living if it wasn't already prepared and ready for you per your contract. Your director or appointed staff will likely give you all the support you need in getting settled with living arrangements. This is another aspect of your transition in which you will need to keep an open mind because your apartment set-up will likely be quite different from your living arrangements back home. It is quite common to see smaller types of apartments in Asia for example, especially in the bigger, more populated Asian cities. It is also not uncommon to see something unusual about the layout and set-up of the apartment. For example, my washer was on the balcony of my apartment in Taiwan, and in my apartment in China, it was conveniently placed below the sink in the kitchen. Also, while you may likely get a washing machine in your apartment, it is unlikely that it will also come with a dryer. Remember, this unique overseas experience goes way beyond a simple dryer in the home, so do not be discouraged. There will be a whole lot more you will be able to experience and achieve on this opportunity that goes beyond the convenience of a dryer. I did not have a dryer in any of my apartments on any of my contracts, but a standing clothes drying rack worked just fine. Get familiar with the types of apartments available in your city and consider whether you will be comfortable with a traditional-style apartment (more cultural look) or a more modern style (like Western apartments). Often, the more modern styles will be a bit more costly than the traditional set-up, however, in general, **you can expect to be paying less in rent** (if not already contracted to be paid by the hiring company) in comparison to what you would pay back home. The only exception was if you were to live in major cities like Tokyo and Abu Dhabi where you will find apartments and the cost of living to be higher.

Begin The Adventure:

- ☐ Call loved ones on arrival
- ☐ Complete arrival paperwork
- ☐ Finalize any additional work visa documents
- ☐ Begin making friends and networking
- ☐ Record the country's emergency numbers
- ☐ Get the address and phone number of your country's consulate in the city
- ☐ Put a translated copy of place of work information or company identification badge in your wallet or pocketbook
- ☐ Make sure Directors/Managers have your emergency contact back home
- ☐ Rest & pace yourself
- ☐ Settle into your new home with an open mind

The International Work Experience

Chapter 5

Surviving Culture Shock

When you finally arrive in another culture and you realize that everything around you may be in a language still unfamiliar to you and others around you do not understand anything you're saying, your first surreal moment of shock is imminent. There is a stark difference between imagining what it would be like and cultivating a preeminent moment of language barrier excitement, and being in the real moment where you realize communication may be a problem and you suddenly ask yourself "OMG, how am I going to survive!"

When making a big move to live in another culture, you will be sure to experience some culture shock, primarily within the first 3 months. Everything from the language to the food to living accommodations and transportation routine and habits will surely take you through an emotional frenzy hopefully with quick adaptation. You will miss home. During the first few weeks, you will automatically compare everything around you to 'how it is back home.' Those who get over culture shock early find and build excitement and appreciation for something new. Those who don't are typically holding on to the frustration of why things aren't the way they are in their home country. As mentioned in Chapter 4, If you want to enjoy your time in any culture, it is pertinent to let go of your cultural norms and be open-minded to embrace someone else's way of life.

The most obvious cultural shock and difference you will experience is the language barrier. But I am here to assure you that you can survive it and appreciate it. Natives will go out of their way to help you and usually with you doing gestures and sign language everything works out fine. From my experience living in Asia for example, if someone did not understand what I was trying to say they would find someone close by who could. Don't worry about anyone being mean to you and ignoring you because you are unable to communicate in their native tongue, this is quite unlikely and very rare. Furthermore, most natives see foreign nationals as an opportunity for them to practice their English skills and will make the effort to try to communicate with you in English. The drawback to that of course, is that it limits your practical use and experience of their native tongue. So, it is up to you to be cognizant of how important it is for you to improve your language skills while living there and thus find a balance between the struggle to communicate and being catered to. In addition, traveling with a small pocket-size translation booklet will always come in handy. For the first couple of days, you may experience fright and frustration but once you start getting the hang of sign language and a few basic words, you will be more at ease. The art of basic vocabulary, speaking slowly, and sign language, goes a long way. If you are on a contract in a country whose language does not use the alphabet system and all the labels on products and signs are in the characters of that language which may be unbeknownst to you, you are most certain to display moments of stillness as you are trapped between hoping to miraculously figure out the writing and guessing what the product is. I referenced this experience earlier when I went to the supermarket in both Taiwan and Mainland China and could not tell the detergent from the softener. Though in circumstances like these, you may experience a moment of shock, once you snap back to reality and seek the help of a store representative using those gestures and signing, you will get closer to resolving what had astonishingly perplexed you for the past few minutes.

    In the last chapter, I previewed what to expect on arrival and touched on what you could anticipate from your living arrangements when I referenced the washing machine being in the kitchen. Well, if you think that's a shock, do not be surprised as you venture on your apartment hunt that you'll see other things out of place from what you're used to. For example, when I was choosing my apartment in China, I viewed an apartment with a shower in the kitchen area. I was puzzled and shocked at the same time and politely declined that apartment and moved on to the next. The next couple of apartments I viewed had much better layouts and so I finally saw one that I said yes to. Be aware though, that as far as a washer set-up goes, it will likely be in the bathroom or kitchen, and as stated before you won't get a dryer but will instead have a clothesline somewhere on the balcony which is very typical of the way of life in both Asia and Europe. As with my apartment in China, and many in other parts of Asia, it will be equipped with a stove but not necessarily an oven, so you will likely have to buy a small countertop oven and get by. You most certainly won't have a dishwasher and expect no floor carpeting or central heating. Wool socks and flannel PJs will become your best friend during those cold chilly months. It is also very typical (and very smart) to see a drain in your bathroom which may or may not be the shower drain as well depending on the set-up. If the bathroom drain is also the shower drain, you will have the unique opportunity of feeling like you a taking a shower in the center of the bathroom. Enjoy!

It is unlikely that you will have to worry about furniture,

as your apartment is likely to be fully furnished with all the necessities. That is, bed, side tables, desk, chair, sofa, TV, coffee table. If something is missing that you think is 'nice to have' you can almost always talk about it with your landlord. Most landlords will try to accommodate your wishes within reason.

One thing that caught my interest while living in Taiwan and Mainland China, was the fact that the food was a bit different from the Chinese food that we are used to in the United States and other parts of the Western world. The best way I can describe this difference is that the food seems lighter in consistency in Asia. You will see noodle dishes for instance, but during my experience, I don't recall seeing much of that heavy Lo mein noodle dish. I also don't recall as many deep-fried meals and one thing that is for certain, it is unlikely, if ever at all, to see a fortune cookie. Nevertheless, same, or different, cookie or no cookie, you still have to eat and a huge part of adjusting to another culture is adjusting to their food. Your diet will change and while you know your limits when it comes to food, I encourage you to be open-minded to trying new things. That's all a part of the experience. In Asia, trying and experiencing a hot pot or 'shabu-shabu' meal is a must! One cultural norm that I appreciated was how there was a collective way of eating and dining rather than an individualistic custom. In U.S. culture for example, when we go out dining as a group, it is very typical and acceptable for each person to order their meal and when it arrives, the server puts that meal directly in front of the person who ordered it. It is further culturally acceptable to now eat just the meal that was served to you unless there is something else that was decided on to be shared, or someone offered to share their dish. Additionally, it is quite acceptable in America and other Western cultures for each person to pay for their meal. In Contrast, in many European and Asian cultures, there is typically more of a collective dining experience the moment there is more than one person dining. That is, it is decided together what meals will be included, when prepared those meals are placed in the center of the table, and each person dining takes a bit from the dishes of choice. At the end of the meal, the bill is divided by the amount of people dining. This was consistently my experience while living in Taiwan and Mainland China, and it was a way of dining that I adjusted to and appreciated.

    As mentioned in Chapter 4, instead of becoming frustrated in the grocery store think of items that are substitutes to still pull off your favorite dish. Dare the adventure of making some of those cultural cuisines as well, and if you will be living in Asia keep chopsticks in your apartment as a way to stay immersed in the culture. Don't worry if you've never used chopsticks before, I guarantee you will get the hang of it when you're really hungry and that's all that's available. You may struggle with chopsticks at every meal for a while, but by the end of your contract, you'll be highly impressed with your almost natural skills in using chopsticks. Though the availability of forks may be limited in certain parts of Asia, you will almost certainly see the availability of major international food franchises like McDonald's and Burger King in many cities and neighborhoods. KFC, Donato's, Pizza Hut, and Starbucks are almost certain to show their faces in most neighborhoods as well, and on some days may just be the pick-me-up needed to relieve your feelings of homesickness.

Unless you took a teaching contract that assigned you to the least metropolitan or somewhat rural cities in countries like Japan, Dakar, or Abu Dhabi for example, where the company may likely provide a car for the convenience of getting to work, you will most likely be taking the local transportation to get back and forth to your job. Rest assured that your apartment will also be in fair proximity to your workplace, whether the company arranged it for you before your arrival or helped you in getting an apartment upon arrival. You therefore can expect to walk to work, jump on the subway, and/or take the city bus. Don't even think about investing in a car on your own, just to recreate or satisfy a way of life that you may be used to back home. It's not worth it. Use this opportunity to explore traveling in ways you hadn't before and to save money for things you wish to do like travel the world and pay off bills or simply to get some extra steps and exercise in. In many cities across the world, it's the way of life to bike to work and school. If you choose to bike it to work and around, don't worry, you'll fit right in. Some Expats who decide to stay overseas beyond a year or two-year contract brave the investment of a scooter bike. In Taiwan, this is a common thing as there will be as many scooters on the road as there are cars. Be cautious though as the cultural norms as they relate to motorists and road rules can be different, daunting, overwhelming, and scary. For example, three weeks after arriving in Taiwan a few friends and I were on our way to a park when we witnessed a local girl get hit by a car off her scooter bike. It was one of the scariest things I've ever witnessed, and we were so bewildered that we put off going to this park for another day.

I recommend similar caution if you are walking or biking to work. **Never assume the rules and customs of the road are the same as in your home country.** Take heed and be extra careful. How you are expected to be treated as a pedestrian back home could be vastly different from what you experience as a pedestrian living in another country. From my experience living in Taiwan and Mainland China, a pedestrian having the walk signal when crossing the street means you have the right-of-way but does not necessarily mean you get the right-of-way. Initially, you will be shocked and terrified, but after a week or so you'll be a pro at maneuvering your way through oncoming cars, buses, and scooters.

      Depending on the city you'll live in, the subways may be overcrowded, especially during rush hour. Seeing the waves of people through the train station and how packed the trains get will shock you, especially if you are coming from a small town in your home country. Even more shocking is to experience pushing and shoving getting on and off the trains. I have witnessed and experienced this during my time living in both Italy and China. If you are expecting a line, you are likely to be in it by yourself and risk getting left by the train. So, I recommend you carefully and politely join in. I will say though that the subway stations and trains across Asia are immaculate with floors so clean you can see your face in them, and subway trains are highly upgraded and maintained. **You will see larger and more advanced rail systems in Europe and Asia**. If you are working in Japan or plan to visit while working in another country be sure to ride the Shinkansen (or bullet train), where your ride will feel like a first-class flight. This was one of the things I looked forward to while staying in Japan, as it is not only one of the fastest trains in the world but also one of the best train travel experiences ever. The Japanese SC Maglev and China's Shanghai Maglev and Fuxing Hao are awe-inspiring experiences as they are regarded as the fastest trains in the world. Other trains in Europe, Saudi Arabia, and Korea also lead the way.

    Traveling by taxi will also likely be your frequent and popular mode of transportation. Taxi drivers are usually friendly and honest with fares. In Mainland China and Taiwan specifically, you will find that a lot of taxi drivers will know some English but there will be many whose English is extremely limited. Be sure to have your address memorized so that you can communicate clearly where you need to go. Sometimes you could merely just show them the written address. Though most taxi drivers are friendly and aim to give you a humble ride, you want to try to not cause the driver confusion with directions and create frustration on either your part and/or theirs. Once you give them the address, they will know how to find it so be mindful that your personally implemented navigation could become a bit overwhelming.

As far as entertainment is concerned there's plenty, so you need not worry about being bored. I will say that although my work had me super busy, I had a lot of fun as far as entertainment during my first overseas contract in Taiwan. I recommend in those moments when homesickness settles in, call a couple of those friends you met during onboarding and hit the town. You will find that your new friends may want to go out so much that you will begin to appreciate some chill and alone time after a while. The point is there will be lots to do and plenty of friends to do it with. You will also find that a common thing for staff to do is to get together and hang out at a nearby local pub after work on a Friday evening. You will soon have your favorite pub as a group as I did with my friends. For example, our 'go-to' pub while living in Taiwan was "0204" in the Banchioa neighborhood of Taipei City. It holds so many good stories and memories for me and my friends.

Entertainment and nightlife will be quite like what you're used to so no shock factor there. The bars and pubs are pretty much the same and, in some respect, you may be shocked at how posh, lit, hyped, and over-the-top the nightclubs are if that's your thing. I must admit, the first time I went to a club in Asia I wasn't sure what to expect. I thought for a while I would be hearing some of the Chinese pop I stumbled onto while browsing through my TV channels in my apartment, but instead, on entering the club I walked in only to hear Jay-Z, Kanye, Beyoncé, Drake, Pitbull, and Naughty by Nature with club dancers on stages dropping the hottest hip hop moves and the bartender doing fire tricks to the beat. It was quite entertaining, and I must say a whole lot of fun. If pubs and clubs aren't your thing, there will be many other things to do from museums to plays, gardens, national and historic parks, malls, concerts, night markets, and visiting numerous cultural and historical sites. Let me also add that while you always want to be careful any time you are out anywhere, whether at home or in a foreign country, **you will feel very safe when going out in many Asian cities (at night or during the day),** and from my personal experience I can attest to that safe feeling while staying in Japan, China, and Taiwan. This level of safety makes it easy and less worrisome to go out and comfortably have fun. Being assured of the safety around you also lessens any hesitation to attend those famous "night markets" so popular throughout Asia. Night markets are awesome, exciting, and a great cultural experience to attend with friends if you wish to hit the town but avoid the clubs. As the name suggests, they are set up and conducted late at night and it is at a night market that you'll most likely be exposed to the most exquisite foods and delicacies of the culture. As a result, a night market experience is a mixture of shock and awe all in one, as it could be completely different from any market experience in your home country but fascinating at the same time.

  Whether you choose to be out at the pub, club, museum, or night market, be prepared for the possibility of encountering and using a squatting toilet when your need for restroom usage arises. That's right, squat toilets, otherwise referred to as squats or squatters, are very common in Asia and can be a huge culture shock. While your apartment is most likely to be equipped with a Western-style toilet, as well as your workplace, many other facilities may have a squatting toilet. I would say the possibility of using a squatter while being out and about in Asia (and from personal testament in Taiwan and Mainland China), is about 50/50. You may be inclined to Google for more vivid imagery; however, I will indulge you with a brief description. Squat toilets lay flat into the tiling of a bathroom floor; therefore, one is unable to physically sit on it but rather has to squat down over it. Your first attempt using a squatter will leave you a bit confused, however, you will figure out fairly quickly which way to turn based on your needs as well as to avoid making or leaving a mess behind. Pretty soon, just as you have assimilated into everything else, you will also be able to use a squat toilet like a pro though comfort with a magazine may seem a bit far-fetched.

A very odd and unique experience that you may encounter when you are out and about, especially in Asia and specifically around highly concentrated cultural and tourism areas, is that of curious stares from local citizens. **You will almost be a celebrity overnight with the fascination local citizens display towards you.** The bigger and more diverse the city the less the fascination and stares, but in general be ready for the attention at some point because you will get it. One of my fondest memories of living and working overseas was the attention received, which occasionally involved the request from a stranger for me to take pictures with them. There were quite a few times when I was out sightseeing or simply going about my daily business when a local stranger would ask to take a picture with me. I was very humbled and thought it to be quite humorous to be receiving this much attention, so I was a good sport and just had fun with it while meeting very nice people in the process. We are all different and understandably someone else may not like this much attention with stares, random conversations, and picture-taking. However, if you find yourself to be the latter, no need to get upset or frustrated, but instead politely decline conversations and pictures and humbly ignore uncomfortable stares. Either way, the important thing to take away from this kind of experience is to understand that the intent is not malicious or negative towards you but is merely a curious fascination for someone they hadn't necessarily had the opportunity to interact with or experience being around in their daily lives. In a nutshell, whether you are in Europe or Asia, being instantly identified and recognized as someone not of the culture is certain. As such, stares of curiosity and amazement will still be forthcoming, though the intensity may lessen depending on the country and the city. Though my emphasis to this point was within regions of Asia, I have experienced this while living in Italy and France as well.

In Chapter 3, I discussed ways to make sure you are prepared for your long-term stay working and living in a foreign country. In doing so, I mentioned being prepared with certain items so that your transition goes smoothly and lowers frustration and that the idea of assuming everything will be readily available to you and to your liking would be a huge overestimation and can result in a great deal of culture shock. Specifically, regarding clothing in Asia, remember it is unlikely to be able to find certain clothing and shoe sizes easily and this can be quite a shock. As I recommended before, you will want to pack wisely and be patient when shopping. This is because most western sizes are not as available in local neighborhood stores but are rather in major malls in the bigger more metropolitan parts of the cities. I also referenced the lack of availability of certain medications in other parts of the world. It can be ridiculously hard to find the specific or similar brand of medication that you may be used to, and this too can be quite a shock. Further, if you do find the same or similar brand of meds, it may not be as strong or have the same effect. In Chinese culture for example herbal medicines are richly preferred, used, and available, as opposed to other forms of medication. While herbal medicines and medicines with lower doses will still serve their purposes, they are a longer and slower process than those quick fixes we may be used to here in Western cultures. Furthermore, in many cultures, the location of a pharmacy may not be as convenient as it is in your culture. For example, here in the U. S., it's very typical to see a small pharmacy in the corner of our neighborhood grocery store or to see a pharmacy within every half mile. In many other cultures getting to a pharmacy may not be as convenient and this could be quite bewildering and shocking. So, throwing a few of those go-to meds in your luggage to get you through the first month or so until you are more familiar with where to go for medication and what is or is not available to you, will surely lessen any anxiety that may develop from this kind of shock.

Remember too in the "Know Before You Go"

chapter, I appealed to female readers by rendering advice on being preemptively prepared with feminine products of your choice, as you may encounter a huge culture shock when you realize your brands of choice are not available, choices available are quite different from what you're used to, or in the case of flushable absorbencies in some parts of Asia, may just be in scarce commodity. While it's natural to experience the greater part of culture shock during your first couple of months living abroad, you may be able to have a greater tolerance and appreciation of the differences in the cultural norms if you are as prepared as you can be for your first few weeks of arrival.

One difference in cultural norms that you will need to adjust to is the rules and laws of that country, which may or may not be strikingly different from those in your home country. Usually, when traveling from one Western culture to another Western culture, you may find some similarities in the way the rules and laws are set up and governed. On the other hand, when traveling from a Western culture to an Eastern culture like in Asia for example, the rules and laws may be strikingly different than those which you are used to. While living within these different rules and laws may contribute to some level of culture shock, it is important to quickly adapt to the mindset that you are in another country with their rules and their laws and not be so quick to put up a challenge. I can recall while living in China a friend of a friend could have gotten himself in some real trouble for challenging an official who was monitoring an outdoor park. The official tried to tell him that he had to exit the park because the park hours were over. These park hours were different from the park hours he was used to back in the United States and so he decided that he wanted more time in the park, because he saw it as ridiculous to close a city park so early and went on to challenge the official. The scene was not pleasant, and after a few words back and forth and a threat to prosecute, he left the park in frustration and rage. As the saying goes, *"When in Rome, do as the Romans do."* It is not worth risking trouble simply because you may be fixated on the way of life you are used to rather than opening your heart and mind to the conformity of another. Remember, **"Attitude is the difference between an ordeal and an adventure" – Bob Bitchin.** Make it an adventure.

How to Minimize Culture Shock:

- *Take a deep breath with the language barrier*
- *Be open-minded about apartment layout*
- *Try new foods, ways of cooking and dining*
- *Use caution with traffic and transportation*
- *Safely do something for fun*
- *Embrace the attention of natives*
- *Obey the rules and laws*

The International Work Experience

Chapter 6

Minding Your Manners

As you settle into the culture and your work, there will be certain things you begin to observe and experience that may not have necessarily been in any book you had bought about the culture, any information you had researched on Google, or anything that you may have learned in your orientation and training. Some of these things are simply patterns and habits that you begin to notice as time goes by, living and working in the culture. Some of these things are also simply being mindful of other's feelings and being professional, respectful, and empathic.
In any of the work opportunities alluded to in this book, you will be working closely in conjunction with local professionals in the same or similar position at your company or school, who will be bilingual in both English and their native language. Those professionals and the staff as a whole are usually delighted that you have joined the company and look forward to the skills and exposure that you bring. They respect you and want to

learn from you. Most often though, the individuals that you will be working closely with or that are a part of your direct team weren't given the convincing work package that was offered to you as the foreign talent coming in. It is therefore extremely important not to discuss or, even worse, to flaunt the benefits that were offered to you in front of them. Most native professionals already have some inclination as to what it took to convince you to hop on a plane and work for their company in a completely different country. Though they may have this knowledge, they remain focused, humbled, grateful, passionate, and professional about their work, and what they bring to the table. They are usually focused on the benefits that they were offered to continue building their career and taking care of themselves and their families. So, they do not need any reminders about what the company or school offered you for work, nor do they need to have such information directly or indirectly thrown in their faces. Frankly, to do so would be unthoughtful, unprofessional, and rude. It is particularly important to mind your manners on certain issues as you would be in a professional position in your home country. Being in a foreign country is not an excuse to simply forget or neglect those professional taboos. I cannot begin to tell you how many times I've single-handedly witnessed such unprofessional and insensitive behavior.

Furthermore, as it relates directly to teaching positions in this sense, most of the native professionals you would be working with will be supporting you in your role immensely. Their tasks and responsibilities are typically extensive as they serve as the cultural and communication liaison to students and/or parents, both in written and verbal form. Being in a role where they are supporting you immensely in addition to having extensive work duties is even more of a reason not to openly discuss your offers and benefits (though you are excited) and be mindful of the fact that you were likely given more of an advantage for fewer responsibilities. It is natural for foreign teachers to gather and talk in excitement about their work opportunities and contracts, and that's fine as long as you remain mindful that those discussions aren't being held around native workers. Be mindful, be professional, and be empathic. Along the same spectrum, I would advise strongly against treating the native professional staff member who is directly supporting you as if they are your secretary. I encourage you to not get into the habit of continuously asking them to do simple things like making your copies and getting you things. They have a job to do and a class to prepare for as well. While what often makes a good successful working team is the ability to support each other, including doing small favors, nice gestures, and lending a helping hand from time to time, to take advantage of someone is completely different and somewhat selfish. They will be very efficient in their role and will stay on top of all their tasks and planning, and I encourage you to do the same so as not to become neglectful or complacent in your duties simply because you realize your local co-teacher or colleague will likely not say no to your requests.

You will observe, especially on a contract in Asia, that there is a genuine, close, and supportive nature in which the native professional staff conduct themselves around each other. They will often sit together, work together, and eat together. There is a supportive and collective nature in which they spend any free time, breaks, or lunchtime. I suggest trying to show some level of comradery and inclusion as well, especially when they try to invite and include you. Typically, when local staff are sitting together in a break room having lunch, for example, they are usually in a comfortable space and so may be speaking in their native language more so than they would at any other time while on duty. I can understand that this may seem discouraging to you, the foreign staff member who may have the intention to be personable and to build a rapport with the native staff. However, simply not speaking or not acknowledging anyone because you may not feel confident around them speaking in their native language or because you may believe there is less you can relate to, would not be the best decision in these circumstances. A simple or friendly statement or two goes a long way. Remember they are bilingual and proficient in English, so don't be afraid to spark a conversation with them or to indulge in one when initiated by them. The point is not to come across as antisocial or distant to a team that you will be working with for a year or more halfway across the world.

    Further, I encourage you to build good relationships with members of the team, because there will likely be instances outside of work that a native staff member will be willing to help you with. I naturally have a very down-to-earth and friendly personality and so with my experiences working overseas, I created great friendships and rich bonds with many members of my team, foreign and native alike. I had great relationships with everyone at the schools and language companies I taught at in Taiwan, France, Italy, and Mainland China. To that extent, if something came up that I needed help figuring out that was non-work related, there were always native staff members who were eager to help me. This is not to say that if you are not friends with the native staff no one will help you when needed. Not at all. This is neither their way nor their culture. They will almost always figure out a way to make sure you get whatever issues you need to be resolved, whether you have a close relationship or not. But having that rapport, especially to a greater level with that one or two people that you bond with, will manifest into having that one or two individuals that you can always count on while living abroad. The native staff want to form friendships and bonds with you as well and will be ready to hang out with you and help out their friends as much as possible. In Taiwan, I became close friends with a native co-worker who was always by my side and ready to help me with anything. In Italy, I could count on my Italian director-friend for any and everything, and in China, my life was much easier because of the bond formed with my assistant teacher. These individuals were there for me through so many moments, from resolving disputes with my home internet company to bringing me food if I'm not feeling well, to holding my hand while I get a tattoo (precious memories). What's even more fulfilling, is that those friendships didn't end on my return home to the U.S., but I still have those life-long friendships with my international friends to this day, some of whom have become like family.

    Be mindful as well of the norms and habits surrounding how business meetings are conducted in the culture you're living in. In some Western cultures and specifically in the United States, it is customary and encouraged to "speak up" in meetings and to have a voice. Doing so in cultures like America reflects positively and shows you are involved and contributing to the team and company. In some Eastern cultures however, speaking up in meetings could be seen as abrasive. You will get a good indication as to the unspoken rules of how meetings are conducted in the culture by about your second or third staff meeting. While working in France and Italy I observed that the professional norms were much like the U.S., where it was highly encouraged to speak up and share my thoughts and ideas. On the other hand, while working in China I quickly observed that most staff members of Chinese descent did not speak during the meetings. Apparently, in Chinese culture, it could come across as rude to always have something to say especially in light of the individual leading the meeting. Rather, it appears that in Chinese culture silence in a meeting signified high respect, wisdom, and intelligence. Speaking up or speaking out would yield quite the opposite and be seen as frivolous, unwise, and of less intelligence. Depending on what you observe in your cultural meetings you may make decisions as to how you choose to conduct yourself personally and professionally. It would be wise to follow the cultural norms and flow, though, in some instances, the expectations of foreign staff to these nuances may be overlooked.

Along these same lines, it is good to be aware of the fact that acknowledging, referencing, or putting a native staff member on the spot in a meeting without them being aware or prepared is something that in some cultures could be a bit bewildering to the person and distasteful in general. Again, **observation, awareness, and respect go a long way.** When you are unsure about certain actions and conduct, first speak with a native supporting staff to get their input and opinion and proceed with grace. It was my observation that in Chinese cultures general things are discussed in a meeting and anything that would bring attention directly to an individual is done privately, whether it is positive or negative. Our Western way of on-the-spot positive acknowledgments or random negative callouts (subtle or brash) is a way of life that could be viewed as arrogant in some Eastern cultures. So be aware, mind your energy and manners, and proceed with caution.

Language barriers and different ways and styles of communicating can cause a lot of meaning and intention to be lost in translation and perception. The native bilingual staff will likely be proficient in English, but it's not their natural birth language and they are speaking English to you within the confines of their culture. It is therefore quite easy for communication to get misunderstood, and you could very well experience a moment where something said directly to you is interpreted to have the wrong tone through the eyes of your Western background culture. In these moments I encourage you not to get upset and react brashly and aggressively, but to pause, take a moment and a deep breath, and extend some grace to your coworker and yourself. Calmly and privately follow up with what was said for clarification. Most often you will find out that how the statement was received was not at all how it was meant but is a result of technically learned language without the proper control of cultural innuendos. In Chinese culture avoiding confrontation is typical. So, it is unlikely that a coworker would intentionally or maliciously say something to you to stir up confrontation and I encourage you to be mindful of a reaction that would do the same. **Remember, having a conversation and having a confrontation are two different things.**

A big part of assimilating into a culture and conforming to its norms is learning about those subtle gestures that are deemed acceptable, unacceptable, or downright offensive. You may have gotten some inclination as to acceptable norms from your preparation and research on the country and culture. Further, usually even if covered briefly, there is some discussion in your onboarding about what to keep in mind while living and functioning in the culture. I did all the above when preparing to embark on each of my overseas work contracts, but there was so much more that I noticed once I began living there. Here are a few things that I can recall from personal experiences from living and working in France, Italy, Taiwan, and Mainland China and from time spent in Japan, which were deemed appropriate, acceptable, or rude and offensive.

In most Asian cultures, and specifically Taiwan and Mainland China where I had some of my experiences, it is very polite to give a subtle bow in acknowledgment of being introduced to someone, when showing respect, and when showing appreciation and gratitude. Handshakes and hugs are typically not a part of Chinese cultural habits and norms and when approached in this manner some individuals may become startled. You will find if such a gesture slips by you if living in the Asian culture, the receiving individual will politely bow a second time or may chuckle and reluctantly and confusingly extend their hand back though they won't necessarily be offended. The respectful bow was something that I adopted very quickly, and I recalled when I returned home to the U.S., I found myself still performing this habit. It took quite some time to start being aware that I was doing this in American culture, and it took me quite some time to get out of it. You will find this to be the case with other behaviors and practices after spending even just a year in another culture, and oddly enough, you may even experience some form of "reverse culture shock" when back home as a result. I also recall that it was impolite to point with a finger in Chinese and Japanese cultures but instead to use your entire hand to gesture and physically refer to that thing or person. Also, when handing something to someone the polite way is to hold the item with both hands instead of one and hand it directly to the person. Never push the item towards the person for them to pick up. A good example of this would be when checking out at the store. In Chinese culture, you will want to hand the money or card to the cashier with both hands. Never give it with one hand and certainly not put it on the counter for the cashier to pick up nor to slide it toward him or her. To do so would be very rude and offensive. Of course, when I returned home, I handed everything over with both hands for at least a year.

It is also not appropriate in Chinese cultures to stare in moments when someone is affected or to draw extra attention to that person or that situation. **"Saving**

face" is a big part of Eastern cultures specifically that of Chinese and Japanese cultures. Earlier in this chapter, I referred to being aware of not putting native staff on the spot in business meetings and not calling them out in any way, positively or negatively. This is an example of saving face. Practicing saving face means not doing anything that will otherwise embarrass someone or cause them to blush awkwardly. In chapter five I talked about experiencing culture shock in Taiwan when I realized how differently traffic operated and when I witnessed a girl being knocked off her scooter bike by a small truck. I remember standing on the side of the road and being shaken up by the accident, so I reacted with high emotions and attention to the incident. My Chinese coworker, who was also with me advised me to be cool and not look at the accident, but to quietly think about the victim as a sign of respect for her and as a way to preserve her dignity and save her face. This occurred three weeks after I arrived in Taiwan, and while I never forgot the incident, what my coworker taught me stuck with me for the remainder of my contract as well, and I was constantly aware and extremely conscientious that I was practicing saving face.

Check Yourself:

- ☐ *Are you keeping the benefits and offers of your contract private?*
- ☐ *Are you Developing relationships with native staff?*
- ☐ *Are you respectful and cognizant of saving face?*
- ☐ *Are you giving yourself and your coworkers grace?*
- ☐ *Are you conforming to acceptable cultural practices?*

The International Work Experience

Conclusion

"Living the Dream"

You've made it! You have embarked on an amazing adventure and opportunity that is a game-changer and life-changer. Appreciate and submerge in every bit of the culture. Use your financial gain to travel like you never had before and save like you never did before. Pay off some financial obligations if that's your intention, enjoy the simple things in life, and make life-long friendships. Remember to be brave and live the dream if it suits you. **Open your mind to opportunities and your heart to possibilities.** Besides taking this brave step in career and cultural exploration, I know of a few friends who were able to take advantage of further international business opportunities or promotions during or after their initial overseas contracts because they opened their minds to opportunities. For example, I had friends who eventually decided to own and run their language school in Taiwan, another friend who was able to expand a career in theatre and produced and directed shows in China, a friend who started a restaurant business in China, and another colleague who took over directing an entire immersive language program in France. I also have at least eight friends who opened their hearts to possibilities and found the magic of love and their romantic partners while teaching overseas. Some of these couples were of the same Western background and some of them were East and West finding each other. At least six of these couples/partners have since married and now have their own families. Financially, a few of my friends paid significantly on their student loans and almost everyone I met who was also on a contract was able to live the dream of visiting a place they hadn't seen before and always wanted to see. For me, while on my contract in Taiwan, my dream was to see the Great Wall of China, and I was able to make that dream come true and fully experience one of the most ancient, historic, and amazing wonders of the world.

"Once you go Global, you won't Stay Local"

A true and resonating phrase for me as seen evident in my second, third, and fourth work-travel contracts. I caught the "travel bug" and it could likely happen to you. There is something so curious and fulfilling about experiencing other parts of the world, different cultures, and seeing amazing cultural and historic sites that just makes you always want to see more. It pulls you in and in some auspicious way becomes a part of who you are. So much so that when you return to your home country, there is a level of discomfort and restlessness that could emerge from feeling as if you should be out in the world doing and experiencing more. This is referred to as "reverse culture shock."

I definitely experienced reversed culture shock when returning to the U.S. from each of my overseas work contracts and you are likely to experience the same. In addition to that sense of feeling as if I should be on the move or out in the world as described above, I certainly had moments of re-inventing the culture I lived in as a way of holding on to the memories and to somewhat reflect my unreadiness to reassimilate back into my own culture. Don't be too amazed if you find yourself in a similar position. As amusing as it might sound, I recall using chopsticks at home for quite some time upon my return to the U.S. after living in Taiwan and Mainland China and also found myself always wanting to dine at a Chinese restaurant. Upon my return, I also felt like my mattress seemed oddly soft and unbearable, and I was overwhelmed by the abundance and availability of so much food, all the time and everywhere. Reverse culture shock is real and somewhat fascinating to think about the irony of it, in that you may have spent a year or two (or more) fitting into another culture only to return to your home country feeling as if you don't quite fit back into yours. But the days will pass, and you will re-assimilate and reintegrate back home just fine while maintaining what is now your natural urge to be a global citizen or nevertheless a globe trotter.

You will be Changed -

Undoubtedly, from the experience of working and living in another culture, you will gain personal growth, greater appreciation of others and culture, international work experience, global connections, career building and advancement, international travel opportunities, some financial comfort, an international friendship network, and invaluable memories. All of these would have contributed to the person you now are and the contributions you now make to a globally changing society.

The International Work Experience

The International Work Experience

In Loving Memory

Curline "Claudette" Grant

The International Work Experience

About The Author

Glaisha Macarius is a Certified Professional Career Coach, Educator, Certified Master Life Coach, Business Owner, and Author. She received her Bachelor of Science in Criminal Justice from Xavier University and her Master of Arts in Interpersonal Communication from Michigan State University, where her research focused on cross-cultural communication.

Within her 12-plus years' experience as an Educator, she's had the unique opportunity to live and teach in Taiwan, France, Italy, and China, as well as to experience travel and recruitment opportunities for Japan. She has a career spanning over 10 years in Career Development where she's assisted many others to acquire, transition, retain, and advance in their careers. Glaisha is the Founder and CEO of Macarius Educational & Career Agency, where in addition to providing educational and career coaching, as a Master Life Coach she supports individuals with navigating through their personal wellness and life goals.

Inspired by her global working experience and career background, she has published "The International Work Experience: A Step-by-Step Guide to Working & Living Overseas", as an inspirational guide to alternative employment opportunities and global experiences, while delivering a personal memoir of her time spent in Taiwan, France, Italy, China, and Japan.

www.ingramcontent.com/pod-product-compliance
Lightning Source LLC
Chambersburg PA
CBHW050012230526
45465CB00003BB/1378